The Best 50

PUMPKIN RECIPES

Marcia Kriner

BRISTOL PUBLISHING ENTERPRISES
Hayward, California

Printed in the United States of America.
ISBN: 1-55867-331-8
Cover design: Frank J. Paredes
Cover photography: John A. Benson
Illustration: Nora Wylde

THE SEASON FOR PUMPKINS

The weather is changing, bringing a chill of autumn to towns and cities everywhere, the leaves turning vibrant reds and oranges, children playing in the yards among freshly fallen leaves. A brisk wind blows over the neighborhoods and a fresh smell of pumpkin pie lingers in the air. It's that time of year again when pumpkins play a part in the best cookies, breads, muffins, and soups.

HISTORY OF A PUMPKIN

The name pumpkin originated from the Greek word for "large melon"—"pepon". The English changed it to "Pumpion". Shakespeare referred to the "pumpion" in his *Merry Wives of Windsor*. American colonists changed the name to "pumpkin".

Native Americans dried strips of pumpkin and wove them into mats. They also roasted long strips of pumpkin on the open fire to

eat. The origin of pumpkin pie occurred when the colonists sliced off the pumpkin top, removed the seeds, and filled the insides with milk, spices and honey. The pumpkin was then roasted in the hot ashes. (They soon found that pumpkins, a fruit native to Americans, make perfect jack o'lanterns, too.)

A TIP – STORE YOUR PIES PROPERLY

Most pumpkin pie recipes contain eggs and/or dairy products. For this reason, the pumpkin pie belongs in your refrigerator. Too often, pies are stored on the counter before and after the big holiday meal. Even commercially prepared pumpkin pie filling has a high proportion of milk and eggs, so it is highly perishable. Keep pumpkin pie — as well as custard pies and other rich egg-laden desserts — hot or cold until ready to serve, then store leftovers in the refrigerator. Fruit pies are safe in the cupboard, pantry shelf, or in a pie keeper on the countertop, for no longer than two days. After that time, the fruit may ferment or mold, spoiling the pie.

PUMPKIN PUREE

Your own fresh pumpkin puree makes better pumpkin breads, pies, soups and other dishes than canned pumpkin. You can use this recipe in almost any recipe in this book that calls for canned pumpkin.

1 large pumpkin (about 3 lb.)

Heat oven to 350°. Cut pumpkin in half and scrape out seeds and threads. Reserve seeds for toasting and snacking. Place halves, cut-side down, on a greased pan. Bake until pumpkin is very tender and can easily be pierced with a fork. A 3 lb. pumpkin takes 1 hour; a smaller pumpkin will take a little less.

Let pumpkin cool. When cool, remove skin and chop flesh into small pieces. Process in a food processor until pureed. Leftover puree can be refrigerated for up to five days, or frozen.

HALLOWEEN DESSERT PUMPKIN PANCAKES

Servings: 4–6

These pancakes can be prepared with butternut squash, Hubbard squash or other varieties of winter squash. Use canned pumpkin or freshly prepared Pumpkin Puree, page 3. *Cold leftover pancakes are an appetizing snack.*

1 cup all-purpose flour
1 tsp. baking powder
1/2 tsp. salt
1 tsp. pumpkin pie spice
1 egg, slightly beaten
2 cups pumpkin puree
1/2 cup molasses or maple syrup

3–4 tbs. buttermilk or milk
2 tbs. unsalted butter or
　　margarine, melted
1/2 cup chopped pecans or
　　hazelnuts, optional
powdered sugar for dusting

In a large bowl, sift together flour, baking powder, salt, and pumpkin pie spice. Set aside.

In another bowl, add egg, pumpkin, molasses, buttermilk and melted butter. Mix until smooth.

Blend in dry ingredients all at once. Mix until batter is smooth. Allow batter to rest for 30 minutes or more. Stir nuts into batter and add an additional tablespoon of buttermilk or milk if batter is too thick.

To make pancakes, spoon 1 heaping tbs. of batter onto a lightly greased, preheated griddle or heavy skillet. With the back of the spoon, flatten batter to about 1/2-inch thickness. Cook slowly until bubbles appear on top and bottom is golden brown. Lift edge to check. Turn and cook until other side is golden brown.

Garnish with powdered sugar or serve with maple syrup.

TOMATO-PUMPKIN SEED DIP

Servings: 6

This party snack could be your next super bowl hit!

1 cup hulled raw pumpkin seeds
1 fresh habañero, serrano or jalapeño chile pepper
2 ripe tomatoes
2 cloves
2 tbs. finely chopped onion
3 tbs. chopped fresh cilantro
salt to taste

In a dry, heavy frying pan, over low heat, toast pumpkin seeds, shaking pan occasionally, until lightly browned, about 8 minutes. Watch carefully that they do not burn. Remove seeds and set aside.

In the same pan, over medium heat, place chile, tomatoes and garlic. Heat, turning occasionally, until well charred—about 3 minutes for garlic, 4 minutes for chile and tomatoes. Remove from heat, cover and set aside to cool.

Place toasted seeds in a spice mill or mini blender and grind to a coarse powder.

Peel tomatoes, coarsely chop and place in a blender or a food processor fitted with a metal blade. Add garlic and process for a few seconds until smooth. Transfer to a serving bowl and stir in ground pumpkin seeds.

Peel chile and cut in half. Remove stem and ribs; if a milder dip is desired, remove seeds as well. Chop finely. Add chile, onion and cilantro to tomato- pumpkin seed mixture. Season to taste with salt. Stir well and serve.

ROASTED PUMPKIN SEEDS

Makes 2 cups

Don't waste pumpkin seeds. When cooked, they make a wonderful, nutritious snack. You can also soak seeds in salted water overnight instead of boiling.

2 cups pumpkin seeds	1 tbs. vegetable oil or melted,
1 qt. water	unsalted butter
2 tbs. salt	

Heat oven to 250°. Pick through seeds and remove the stringy fibers. Bring water and salt to a boil. Add seeds and boil for 10 minutes. Drain. Spread on a kitchen towel or paper towel and pat dry.

Place seeds in a bowl and toss with oil or butter. Spread evenly on a large cookie sheet. Place pan in oven and roast seeds for 30 to 40 minutes. Stir about every 10 minutes, until crisp and golden brown. Cool and shell seeds. Store in an airtight container.

PUMPKIN CHEESE BALL

Makes: 3 cups

No one will guess this make-ahead spread has pumpkin in it, but that subtle ingredient lends harvest color and some nutrition.

1 pkg. (8 oz.) cream cheese, softened
1/2 cup canned or cooked pumpkin
1 can (8 oz.) crushed pineapple, well drained
1 tbs. finely chopped onion

2 cups (8 oz.) shredded sharp cheddar cheese
1 pkg. (2 1/2 oz.) dried beef, finely chopped
celery leaves
crackers and/or raw vegetables

In a bowl, beat cream cheese, pumpkin and pineapple. Stir in onion, cheddar cheese and beef. Shape into a ball; place on a serving platter. Score sides with a knife to resemble a pumpkin and add celery leaves for a stem. Serve with crackers and/or vegetables.

FROSTED PUMPKIN DOUGHNUTS

Makes: about 3 dozen

During harvest is the time to make these scrumptious doughnuts. The orange frosting makes the perfect yummy icing.

2 eggs
1 cup sugar
2 tbs. butter or margarine, softened
1 cup cooked or canned pumpkin
1 tbs. lemon juice
4½ cups all-purpose flour
2 tsp. baking powder
1 tsp. baking soda

½ tsp. salt
½ tsp. cinnamon
½ tsp. nutmeg
1 cup evaporated milk
oil for deep frying
3 cups confectioners' sugar
2–3 tbs. orange juice
1 tbs. evaporated milk
1 tsp. grated orange peel

In a bowl, beat eggs, sugar and butter. Add pumpkin and lemon juice; mix well. Combine flour, baking powder, baking soda, salt, cinnamon and nutmeg; add to pumpkin mixture alternately with milk. Cover and refrigerate for 2 hours. Turn onto a lightly floured surface. Knead 5 or 6 times. Roll to 3/8-inch thickness. Cut with a 2 1/2-inch doughnut cutter.

In an electric skillet or deep-fat fryer, heat oil to 375°. Fry doughnuts, a few at a time, until golden, about 3 minutes. Turn once with a slotted spoon. Drain on paper towels.

For Frosting, combine confectioners' sugar, orange juice, evaporated milk and orange peel. Spread mixture over cooled doughnuts.

PUMPKIN BANANA NUT BREAD

Makes: 2 loaves

The combination of bananas and pumpkin creamed together along with just the right amount of spices make this an impressive bread. You'll want to make this several times a year.

4 cups all-purpose flour
4 tsp. baking powder
2 tsp. pumpkin pie spice
4 tsp. cinnamon
1 tsp. nutmeg
½ tsp. ground ginger
2 tsp. baking soda
½ tsp. salt
1 can (15oz.) pumpkin

4 large eggs
1 tsp. vanilla
1 cup granulated sugar
1 cup brown sugar, packed
1 cup (medium) very ripe
  bananas, mashed
¾ cup vegetable oil
1 cup chopped walnuts

Heat oven to 350°. Grease and flour two 9 x 5-inch loaf pans. Combine flour, baking powder, pumpkin pie spice, cinnamon, nutmeg, ginger, baking soda, and salt in a medium bowl.

Combine pumpkin, eggs, vanilla, granulated sugar, brown sugar, bananas and vegetable oil in a large bowl; beat until smooth. Gradually beat in flour mixture. Stir in nuts. Spoon into prepared loaf pans.

Bake for 55 to 60 minutes, or until a wooden pick inserted in the center comes out clean. Cool in pans on wire racks for 10 minutes; remove to wire racks to cool completely.

PUMPKIN BREAD

Makes: 2 loaves

Try sprinkling brown sugar and walnuts on top before baking this.

3½ cups all-purpose flour
2 tsp. baking soda
1 tsp. salt
1 tsp. cinnamon
1 tsp. nutmeg
3 cups sugar
1 cup vegetable oil

4 eggs, beaten
¾ cup buttermilk
1 tsp. butter flavoring
1 tsp. vanilla extract
1 can (16 oz.) pumpkin
1 cup raisins
1 cup chopped pecans

In a large bowl, sift together flour, baking soda, salt, cinnamon and nutmeg. Add sugar, oil, eggs and buttermilk. Mix well. Stir in butter flavoring, vanilla, pumpkin, raisins and pecans. Pour into two greased 9 x 5-inch loaf pans. Bake at 350° for 60 to 65 minutes, or until bread tests done. Let stand for 10 minutes before removing from pans. Cool on a wire rack. Sprinkle with confectioners' sugar.

PUMPKIN BREAD WITH APPLESAUCE

Makes: 3 loaves

Applesauce gives this bread an extra rich and moist flavor.

3½ cups all-purpose flour
2 tsp. baking soda
1 tsp. salt
½ tsp. baking powder
3 cups white sugar
1 tsp. cinnamon

1 tsp. pumpkin pie spice
1 cup applesauce
4 eggs
1 can (15 oz.) pumpkin
¼ cup water
½ cup chopped walnuts, optional

Grease three loaf pans. Heat oven to 350°. In a large bowl, combine flour, baking soda, salt, baking powder, sugar, cinnamon and pumpkin pie spice. Stir well. Add applesauce, eggs, pumpkin and water. Mix batter with a mixer. Stir in nuts.

Pour batter into prepared pans. Bake for 50 to 60 minutes, until tester inserted in center comes out clean.

PUMPKIN CHOCOLATE CHIP BREAD

Makes: 1 loaf

This recipe was used for children in a local kindergarten. They loved the chocolate chips! For a different flavor, try using dried orange peel or dried cranberries instead of chocolate chips.

½ cup butter or margarine, softened
1 cup sugar
2 eggs
1¼ cups canned pumpkin
2 cups all-purpose flour
1 tsp. baking soda

1 tsp. cinnamon
½ tsp. nutmeg
½ tsp. pumpkin pie spice
¼ tsp. ground cloves
¼ tsp. ground ginger
¼ cup chocolate chips
¼ cup chopped walnuts

GLAZE
1 tbs. heavy cream
½ cup confectioners' sugar

In a large bowl, cream butter. Gradually add sugar, eggs and pumpkin.

In a separate bowl, combine flour, baking soda, cinnamon, nutmeg, pumpkin pie spice, cloves and ginger. Stir dry ingredients into creamed mixture and blend well. Stir in chocolate chips and walnuts.

Pour into a greased, floured 9 x 5-inch loaf pan. Bake at 350° for 45 to 50 minutes, or until loaf tests done. Cool on a wire rack.

For glaze, combine heavy cream and sugar and drizzle over cooled bread.

PUMPKIN CRANBERRY BREAD

Makes: 2 loaves

This bread is wonderfully moist, and the cranberries are an added bonus. Since the recipe makes two loaves, it is perfect for sharing with a neighbor or friend.

3 cups all-purpose flour
1 tbs. plus 2 tsp. pumpkin pie spice
2 tsp. baking soda
1½ tsp. salt
3 cups granulated sugar
1 can (15 oz.) pumpkin or 2 cups *Pumpkin Puree,* page 3
4 large eggs
1 cup vegetable oil
½ cup orange juice or water
1 cup sweetened dried, fresh or frozen cranberries

Heat oven to 350°. Grease and flour two 9 x 5-inch loaf pans. Combine flour, pumpkin pie spice, baking soda and salt in a large bowl. Combine sugar, pumpkin, eggs, oil and juice in a large bowl; beat until just blended.

Add pumpkin mixture to flour mixture; stir just until moistened. Fold in cranberries. Spoon batter into prepared loaf pans. Bake for 60 to 65 minutes, or until a wooden pick inserted in the center comes out clean. Cool in pans on a wire rack for 10 minutes; remove to wire rack to cool completely.

FOR THREE 8 X 4-INCH LOAF PANS

Prepare as above. Bake for 55 to 60 minutes.

FOR FIVE OR SIX 5 X 3-INCH MINI-LOAF PANS

Prepare as above. Bake for 50 to 55 minutes.

PUMPKIN NUT BREAD

Makes: 1 large or 2 mini loaves

This, of course, is an old family favorite; it makes a great snack, breakfast or dessert; is great for giving as a gift; and it freezes well, too—just wrap carefully in aluminum foil.

2 cups flour, or 1 cup each
   whole wheat flour and
   all-purpose flour
2 tsp. baking powder
1/2 tsp. baking soda
1 tsp. cinnamon
1/2 tsp. salt
1/2 tsp. nutmeg
1 cup *Pumpkin Puree,* page 3,

   or canned pumpkin
1 cup sugar
1/2 cup skim milk
2 eggs slightly beaten
1/4 cup vegetable oil
1/2 cup each: chopped pecans
   and black walnuts (may
   substitute raisins)

SNACKS, BREADS AND BREAKFASTS

Heat oven to 350°. Sift together flour, baking powder, baking soda, cinnamon, salt and nutmeg.

In a large bowl, combine pumpkin, sugar, milk and eggs. Mix well. Add dry ingredients, oil and nuts. Mix just until moistened. Batter will be slightly lumpy. Do not overmix. Spoon batter into a well-greased 9 x 5-inch loaf pan or two 7½ x 3¾-inch loaf pans. Bake in middle of oven. For a large loaf, cook for 65 minutes; for two mini loaves, cook for 50 minutes, or until a wooden pick inserted in the center comes out clean.

Cool for 10 minutes in pan. Run a knife around edges of pan to loosen bread from pan. Then turn bread over and cool on a cooling rack.

PUMPKIN SCONES WITH BERRY BUTTER

Makes: 12

These scones are packed with dried berries and spices.

2¼ cups all-purpose flour
¼ cup brown sugar, packed
2 tsp. baking powder
1½ tsp. pumpkin pie spice
¼ tsp. baking soda
¼ tsp. salt
½ cup chilled butter or
   margarine
1 large egg, beaten

½ cup canned pumpkin
⅓ cup milk
Berry Butter
2 tbs. dried cranberries or dried
   blueberries
½ cup boiling water
½ cup margarine or butter,
   softened
3 tbs. powdered sugar

Heat oven to 400°. In a bowl, combine flour, brown sugar, baking powder, pumpkin pie spice, baking soda and salt. With a pastry blender, cut in chilled butter until mixture resembles coarse crumbs.

Make a well in center of dry mixture; set aside.

In another bowl, combine egg, pumpkin and milk. Add egg mixture all at once to dry mixture. Using a fork, stir just until moistened. Turn out dough onto a lightly floured surface. Quickly knead dough by folding and pressing gently for 10 to 12 strokes, or until nearly smooth. Pat dough into an 8-inch circle. Cut into 12 wedges. Arrange wedges on an ungreased baking sheet. If desired, brush tops with additional milk. Bake for 12 to 15 minutes, or until golden. Remove scones from baking sheet and cool on a wire rack for 5 minutes. Serve warm with *Berry Butter.*

To make *Berry Butter,* in a small bowl, combine dried cranberries and boiling water. Let stand for 10 minutes. Drain well and finely chop berries. Stir together margarine, powdered sugar, and cranberries. Cover and chill for at least 1 hour before serving, to allow flavors to blend.

WHOLE-WHEAT PUMPKIN BREAD

Makes: 2 loaves

This bread tastes fantastic toasted with a spread of pumpkin apple butter! The whole wheat and cornmeal give this bread a very unique texture.

2½ cups (12½ oz.) whole-wheat flour
½ cup (2½ oz.) yellow or white cornmeal
2 tbs. baking soda
1 tsp. ground ginger
1½ tsp. cinnamon
½ tsp. ground cloves
½ tsp. nutmeg
½ tsp. salt

⅔ cup unsalted butter, room temperature
2 cups sugar
2 cups *Pumpkin Puree,* page 3, or canned pumpkin
4 eggs
⅔ cup water
1 cup raisins
½ cup chopped walnuts

Heat oven to 350°. Grease and flour 2 medium 8½-inch loaf pans.

In a medium bowl, stir and toss together flour, cornmeal, baking soda, ginger, cinnamon, cloves, nutmeg and salt. Set aside.

In a large bowl, beat together butter and sugar until blended; a hand-held mixer is useful for this step. Beat in pumpkin, eggs and water. Add combined dry ingredients and beat just until blended. Stir in raisins and walnuts.

Pour into prepared pans and bake until a thin wooden skewer inserted in the center comes out clean, about 60 to 65 minutes. Let cool in pans for 10 minutes, then turn out onto a wire rack to cool completely.

PUMPKIN YEAST BREAD-MACHINE BREAD

Makes: 1 loaf

This bread has a crisp brown crust and golden orange interior.

½ cup plus 2 tbs. warm water
½ cup cooked or canned
   pumpkin
¼ cup butter or margarine,
   softened
¼ cup instant nonfat dry
   milk powder

¼ cup brown sugar, packed
1 tsp. cinnamon
½–1 tsp. nutmeg
¾ tsp. salt
⅛ tsp. ground ginger
2¾ cups bread flour
1 pkg. (¼ oz.) active dry yeast

In the bread machine pan, place all ingredients in the order suggested by manufacturer. Select basic bread setting. Choose crust color and loaf size if available. Bake according to bread machine directions. Check dough after 5 minutes of mixing; add 1 to 2 tbs. of water or flour if needed.

PUMPKIN APPLE BUTTER

Makes: 3 cups

Fresh bread spread with homemade apple butter (with pumpkin as the base) is a rich treat!

1 can (15 oz.) pumpkin or 2
  cups *Pumpkin Puree*, page 3
1 cup apple, peeled and grated
1 cup apple juice

½ cup brown sugar, packed
¾ tsp. pumpkin pie spice
buttermilk biscuits, bread, corn
  muffins or cereal for serving

Combine pumpkin, apple, apple juice, sugar and pumpkin pie spice in a medium, heavy-duty saucepan. Bring to a boil; reduce heat to low.

Cook, stirring occasionally, for 1½ hours. Serve with buttermilk biscuits, bread, corn muffins or hot cereal. Store in an airtight container in the refrigerator for up to 2 months.

BEEF STEW IN A PUMPKIN

Servings: 4

When the weather is cold, this is a perfect tummy warmer.

1 sugar pumpkin or butternut
  squash, about 5 lb.
1 tbs. vegetable oil
1 lb. beef top round, fat trimmed,
  cut into ½ inch cubes
1¾ cups (14 oz.) beef stock
1 tbs. butter or margarine
3 yellow onions, halved, in

½-inch-thick slices
3 small parsnips, peeled and
  coarsely chopped
½ tsp. cinnamon
½ tsp. nutmeg
¼ cup bourbon or any whiskey
2 tbs. brown sugar
salt and freshly ground pepper

Heat oven to 350°. Cut around stem of pumpkin or squash and discard stem or set aside to use as a lid. Scoop out and discard seeds. Line bottom and sides of a shallow baking pan with aluminum foil and spray with cooking spray or grease with vegetable

oil. Place pumpkin or squash in baking pan and set aside.

In a 4-quart, heavy-bottomed pot, over medium-high heat, warm vegetable oil. Add beef cubes and brown well on all sides, about 5 minutes. Transfer beef to a dish. Pour beef stock into pot and, over medium-high heat, stir to dislodge browned bits from bottom of pot. Pour liquid over beef.

In the same pot, over medium heat, melt butter. Add onions and parsnips. Sauté, stirring, until onions are browned lightly, about 15 minutes. Return beef and juices to pot. Add cinnamon, nutmeg and bourbon. Mix well, then spoon beef mixture into pumpkin. Sprinkle brown sugar over. Bake until pumpkin is soft when pierced with a fork, and meat is tender, about 2 to $2\frac{1}{2}$ hours. About 45 minutes before stew is done, place pumpkin top, if using, on a baking sheet and bake until tender, about 45 minutes.

Season stew to taste with salt and pepper. Top with pumpkin lid. Spoon into warmed bowls and serve immediately.

ITALIAN PUMPKIN STRATA

Serves: 12

This is a delicious casserole you can cut into squares or wedges and serve with a platter of fresh fruit for a smashing brunch!

1 tbs. vegetable oil
1 lb. sweet Italian sausage, casings removed
1 small onion, chopped
1/2 cup chopped green bell pepper
1/2 cup chopped red bell pepper
2 cloves garlic, finely chopped
12 cups (1 1/2-inch cubes) Italian or French bread
2 cups shredded mozzarella

2 cans (12 oz. cans) evaporated milk
1 can (15 oz.) pumpkin or 2 cups *Pumpkin Puree,* page 3
4 large eggs
1 tsp. salt
1/2 tsp. ground black pepper
1/2 tsp. dried oregano, crushed
1/2 tsp. dried basil, crushed
1/2 tsp. dried marjoram, crushed

Heat oven to 350°. Grease a 9 x 13-inch baking pan. Heat oil in a large skillet, over medium-high heat. Add sausage, onion, bell peppers and garlic. Cook, stirring to break up sausage, for 7 to 10 minutes, or until sausage is no longer pink; drain.

In a large bowl, combine bread cubes, cheese and sausage mixture. In a medium bowl, heat evaporated milk, pumpkin, eggs, salt, pepper, oregano, basil and marjoram.

Pour pumpkin mixture over bread mixture, stirring gently to moisten bread. Pour into prepared baking pan. Bake for 30 to 35 minutes, or until set. Serve warm.

TAGLIATELLE WITH PUMPKIN AND SAGE

Serves:4

This dish is something to try, if you are a lover of pasta. The different taste of a pumpkin sauce will amaze you and no doubt be a big hit with family and friends.

1 piece pumpkin (about 1 lb.)
1/3 cup unsalted butter
1 white onion, sliced paper-thin
8 fresh sage leaves
1 lb. dried spinach tagliatelle or fettuccine (or 3/4 lb. fresh)
3/4 cup (3 oz.) freshly grated parmesan cheese
salt and freshly ground white pepper to taste

Peel pumpkin; remove seeds and strings and discard. Cut pumpkin into small cubes; you should have about 3 cups. Set aside.

In a large frying pan, over medium heat, melt half of the butter. Add onion and saute, stirring, until translucent. Add pumpkin and cook, stirring often, until tender, about 20 minutes longer.

When pumpkin is almost ready, melt remaining butter in another frying pan over medium-high heat. Add sage leaves and fry until slightly crisp, just 1 or 2 minutes.

Meanwhile, in a large pot, bring 5 quarts of salted water to a boil. Add pasta and cook until tender. Drain and transfer to a warmed serving dish. Immediately pour pumpkin sauce over pasta. Add parmesan, salt and white pepper and toss well. Pour sage and butter over pasta and serve at once.

PUMPKIN SOUP

Serves: 8

If you have never tried pumpkin soup, you are in for a real treat. This is the best winter soup to warm you up.

6 cups chicken stock
1½ tsp. salt
3½ cups chopped, cubed fresh pumpkin
1 cup chopped onion

½ tsp. chopped fresh thyme
1 clove garlic, minced
5 whole black peppercorns
½ cup heavy whipping cream
1 tsp. fresh parsley

Heat stock, salt, pumpkin, onion, thyme, garlic and peppercorns. Bring to a boil, reduce heat to low, and simmer for 30 minutes, uncovered. Puree mixture in a blender or food processor. Return to pot and bring to a boil again. Reduce heat to low and simmer for another 30 minutes, uncovered. Stir in heavy cream. Pour into soup bowls and garnish with fresh parsley.

PUMPKIN AND GORGONZOLA SOUP

Serves: 4

This soup is very easy and hearty: the gorgonzola cheese gives it just a bit of tang.

1 can (15 oz.) pumpkin or 2 cups *Pumpkin Puree*, page 3
1½ cups water
2 tsp. instant chicken flavor bouillon
1 tsp. ground sage

12 oz. evaporated milk
¾ cup crumbled Gorgonzola cheese
1 large green onion, finely chopped, for garnish
black pepper for seasoning

Cook pumpkin, water, bouillon and sage in a large saucepan, stirring frequently, until mixture comes to a boil. Stir in evaporated milk and cheese. Reduce heat to low. Cook, stirring frequently, until most of cheese is melted. Sprinkle with green onion before serving. Season to taste with ground black pepper.

CURRIED PUMPKIN SOUP

Servings: 4

This tasty dish has very little sugar, salt or fat.

1 small onion, chopped
1 tsp. cooking oil
2 cups chicken broth
1½ cups *Pumpkin Puree*, page 3, or canned pumpkin
1 tbs. lemon juice
1 tsp. curry powder
1 tsp. sugar
½ tsp. salt, optional
1 dash pepper
½ cup half-and-half, cream, or evaporated milk
chopped fresh parsley for garnish, optional

In a saucepan, over medium heat, saute onion in oil until tender. Add broth, pumpkin, lemon juice, curry powder, sugar, salt (if desired) and pepper; bring to a boil.

Reduce heat; cover and simmer for 15 minutes. Stir in half-and-half; heat through. Garnish with parsley if desired.

PLAIN PASTRY

Makes two 9-inch pie crusts

If only 1 shell is needed, roll out the other and freeze until needed.

2 cups sifted flour
¾ tsp. salt
⅔ cups shortening or butter,
softened
4–6 tbs. cold water

Sift flour and salt together. Cut in shortening with 2 knives or a pastry blender. Add water, using only small amounts at a time, until mixture holds together. If using butter, refrigerate dough until cold. Divide dough into 2 parts. Roll out on floured board to desired size. Line a pie pan with 1 piece of dough, being careful not stretch dough. After filling is placed in pastry, dampen edges of lower crust with cold water. Cover with remaining dough. Slash in several places to allow steam to escape while baking. Press edges together with the prongs of a fork or flute edges. Bake according to recipe for filling selected.

DOUBLE LAYER PUMPKIN PIE

The double layer of pumpkin and the soft delicacy of cream cheese at the bottom

1 pkg. (12 oz.) cream cheese, softened
1 tbs. milk
1 tbs. sugar
1½ cups frozen, non-dairy whipped topping
1 purchased, ready crust graham cracker piecrust
1 cup cold milk
1 pkg. (4-serving size) vanilla flavor instant pudding and pie filling
1 can (16oz.) pumpkin
2 tsp. pumpkin pie spice

Mix cream cheese, 1 tbs. milk and sugar in a large bowl with a wire whisk until smooth. Gently stir in whipped topping.

Spread on bottom of prepared pie crust. Pour 1 cup milk into bowl. Add pudding mix. Beat with a wire whisk for 1 minute. Mixture will be thick. Stir in pumpkin and spice with wire whisk, until well mixed. Spread over cream cheese layer.

Refrigerate for 4 hours, or until set. Garnish with additional whipped topping. Refrigerate leftovers.

HOMEMADE PUMPKIN PIE

Makes one 9-inch pie

The traditional holiday pumpkin pie has been around since the 1950s. It's easy to make: just mix, pour and bake. Serve with ice cream or whipped cream for topping.

1/8 tsp. salt
3/4 cup sugar
2 tbs. brown sugar
2 tsp. pumpkin pie spice
1/4 tsp. nutmeg

2 eggs, slightly beaten
2/3 cup milk
1 1/2 cups *Pumpkin Puree,* page 3
1 crust *Plain Pastry,* page 37
nutmeg for topping

Sift salt, sugars, spice and nutmeg together; stir into eggs. Add milk and pumpkin and combine. Line a 9-inch pie pan with pastry and pour in filling. Sprinkle with nutmeg. Bake at 450° for 10 minutes. Reduce temperature to 325° and bake for about 35 minutes, until a knife inserted in the center comes out clean. Cool.

QUICK CREAMY PUMPKIN PIE

Servings: 8

Vanilla pie filling and non-dairy topping make this pie so light and fluffy it'll have your guests coming back for seconds.

½ cup cold milk
1 pkg. (6-serving size) vanilla
   flavor instant pudding and pie
   filling
1 tsp. pumpkin pie spice

1 cup canned pumpkin
1½ cups frozen non-dairy
   whipped topping, thawed
1 purchased graham cracker
   piecrust

In a large bowl, beat milk, pudding mix and spice with a wire whisk for 1 minute. Mixture will be very thick. Whisk in pumpkin and stir in whipped topping. Spread in crust. Refrigerate for at least 2 hours, or until set. Garnish as desired. Store in refrigerator.

You may substitute ½ tsp. cinnamon, ¼ tsp. ground ginger, and ⅛ tsp. ground cloves in place of pumpkin pie spice.

PUMPKIN APPLE PIE

This makes a wonderful combination for an autumn day. Now you don't have to choose between apple and pumpkin pie.

1 crust *Plain Pastry*, page 37
2 medium apples (Granny Smith or pippin)
1 tsp. butter
2 cups *Pumpkin Puree,* page 3, or canned pumpkin
1½ cups light cream or half-and-half
1 cup brown sugar
2 eggs
1 tsp. cinnamon
½ tsp. nutmeg
¼ tsp. ground cloves
¼ tsp. ground ginger

Heat oven to 425°. Grease a 10-inch pie plate. Roll out pastry to fit pie pan. Trim and flute edges. Refrigerate.

Peel, core, and cut apples into ¼-inch slices. Place in a skillet with butter, cover, and cook over low heat for 5 minutes. Remove and drain apples.

Place pumpkin, cream, sugar, eggs and spices in a medium bowl. Beat together until smooth. Arrange apple slices in bottom of the chilled pastry shell. Pour pumpkin mixture over apples. Sprinkle top with a dash of nutmeg.

Bake for 15 minutes at 425°. Reduce oven to 375° and bake for 35 to 40 minutes, or until a knife inserted into the center comes out clean. Allow to cool. Serves 8 to 10.

PUMPKIN CHIFFON PIE

Servings: 8

If you are pressed for time making this pie, you can use a ready-made 9-inch graham cracker pie shell for the crust.

1 can (15 oz.) pumpkin or 2
   cups *Pumpkin Puree,* page 3
1½ cups sugar
½ tsp. salt
1 tsp. cinnamon
¼ tsp. cloves
¼ tsp. nutmeg
¼ tsp. ginger

3 tbs. rum
1½ cups heavy whipping cream
1 cup flour
2 tbs. sugar
½ tsp. salt
6 tbs. butter
1–2 tbs. water

In a large bowl, blend pumpkin, sugar, salt, spices and rum. Whip cream with a blender until stiff peaks form. Fold two-thirds of the cream into pumpkin mixture. Turn into pastry shell. Freeze until firm.

Top with remaining whipped cream and return to freezer.

For pastry shell, mix flour, sugar and salt. Cut in butter. Mix in water to form dough. Pull off a small piece of dough and roll out on floured board. Cut out 2 or 4 leaf shapes.

Roll out remaining dough and fit into a 9-inch pan, 2 to 3 inches deep. Prick with tines of fork. Bake in a 400° oven for 15 minutes, or until golden brown. Bake leaves in shallow pan just until golden. Cool. Top pie with your cut out leaves.

If you are pressed for time, you can use a ready-made 9-inch graham cracker pie shell.

PUMPKIN GINGERBREAD PIE

Servings: 8

Adding gingerbread mix gives this pie a nice swirled look.

1 cup canned pumpkin
⅓ cup sugar
1 tsp. pumpkin pie spice
1 slightly beaten egg

½ cup half-and-half
1 pkg. (14.5 oz.) gingerbread mix
nonstick cooking spray
whipped cream, optional

Heat oven to 350°. In a small bowl, combine pumpkin, sugar and pumpkin pie spice. Add egg. Beat lightly with a rotary beater or fork, just until combined. Gradually stir in half-and-half; mix well. Prepare gingerbread mix according to package directions. Coat an 8 x 8-inch baking dish with cooking spray. Pour batter into prepared dish. Lightly spoon pumpkin mixture over gingerbread batter; swirl gently using a table knife. Bake for 60 minutes, or until a pick inserted in gingerbread portion comes out clean. Cool slightly. Serve warm or at room temperature with whipped cream.

PUMPKIN-PECAN PIE

Servings: 8

For a nice presentation, cut out leaves from a piece of dough. Bake with the pie, and place around edges of the baked pie.

1 crust *Plain Pastry,* page 37	¼ cup rum
1½ cups (12 oz.) canned pumpkin	1 tsp. cinnamon
½ cup pecan halves, toasted	1 tsp. ground ginger
4 eggs	1 tsp. ground cloves
¾ cup sugar	1½ cups heavy cream

Heat oven to 425°. Combine pumpkin and pecans in a food processor fitted with a metal blade. Process until smooth and well blended. Scrape into a bowl. Beat in eggs and add sugar, rum and spices. Blend well. Add cream and stir until completely mixed.

Fit pastry in a 9-inch pie pan. Pour pumpkin into pan. Bake for 10 minutes. Reduce heat to 300° and bake for about 40 minutes, until a knife inserted in the center comes out clean.

PUMPKIN PUDDING PIE

I make this super easy pudding year-round, when I have no time for baking. I put this in the slow cooker, and I have a delicious dessert at the end of the day—pumpkin pie without the crust.

1 can (15 oz.) pumpkin or 2
　cups *Pumpkin Puree,* page 3
1 can (12oz.) evaporated milk
¾ cup sugar
½ cup biscuit/baking mix
2 eggs, beaten

2 tbs. butter or margarine,
　melted
2½ tsp. pumpkin pie spice
2 tsp. vanilla extract
whipped topping, optional

In a large bowl, combine all ingredients except topping. Transfer to a slow cooker coated with nonstick cooking spray.

Cover and cook on low for 6 to 7 hours, or until a thermometer reads 160°. Serve in bowls with whipped topping if desired.

INDIVIDUAL PUMPKIN CUSTARDS

Servings: 4

This is a nice variation on pumpkin pie, and a cinch to prepare.

1 can (15 oz.) pumpkin
2 large eggs
1 cup half-and-half
1/4 cup brown sugar, packed
1 tsp. cinnamon

1 1/2 tsp. pumpkin pie spice
1/2 tsp. salt
1/4 cup brown sugar, packed
1/4 cup chopped pecans
1 tbs. butter, melted

Heat oven to 350°. In a bowl, combine pumpkin, eggs, half-and-half, brown sugar, spices and salt. Beat until smooth. Pour into 4 greased, 10 oz. custard cups. Place in a 9 x 13-inch baking pan; pour hot water around cups to a depth of 1 inch. Bake, uncovered, at 350° for 20 minutes. Meanwhile, in a small bowl, combine brown sugar, pecans and butter. Sprinkle over custard. Bake for 30 to 35 minutes longer, until a knife inserted near the center comes out clean. Serve warm or chilled.

GINGERSNAP PUMPKIN MOUSSE TORTE

Pecan halves and a drizzle of caramel ice cream topping grace the top of this rich, creamy dessert.

1½ cup finely crushed gingersnaps

1 cup finely chopped, toasted pecans

⅓ cup margarine or butter, melted

½ cup sugar

1 envelope unflavored gelatin

½ cup light cream or half-and-half

3 large, beaten egg yolks

¼ cup water

1 can (15 oz.) pumpkin or 2 cups *Pumpkin Puree*, page 3

2 tsp. pumpkin pie spice

4 oz. (½ container) frozen whipped dessert topping, thawed

½ cup pecan halves, toasted

¼ cup caramel ice cream topping

Mix gingersnaps, chopped pecans and margarine. Press onto bottom and 1½ inches up sides of an 8-inch springform pan Or, press into a 9-inch pie plate. Bake in a 350° oven for 10 to 12 minutes, or until edge is golden. Cool.

In a saucepan, mix sugar and gelatin. Stir in cream, egg yolks, and water. Cook and stir over low heat until gelatin is dissolved and mixture just begins to bubble. Remove from heat. Stir in pumpkin and spice. Let cool for 20 to 30 minutes.

Fold dessert topping into gelatin mixture. Spread evenly in crust. Top with pecan halves. Cover and chill for 6 hours, or until set. Loosen sides of pan. You can cover and chill for up to 24 hours. Drizzle with ice cream topping.

PUMPKIN CHEESECAKE

Servings: 16

This rich and creamy dessert features a unique pumpkin and cream cheese combination, with a smooth texture and irresistible graham cracker crust.

1½ cups graham cracker crumbs
⅓ cup butter or margarine, melted
¼ cup granulated sugar
1½ lb. cream cheese, softened
1 cup granulated sugar
¼ cup light brown sugar, packed
2 large eggs
1 can (15 oz.) pumpkin or 2 cups *Pumpkin Puree,* page 3

⅔ cup (5 oz. can) evaporated milk
2 tbs. cornstarch
1¼ tsp. cinnamon
½ tsp. nutmeg
16 oz. sour cream, at room temperature
⅓ cup granulated sugar
1 tsp. vanilla extract

Heat oven to 350°. Combine graham cracker crumbs, butter and granulated sugar in a medium bowl. Press onto bottom and 1 inch up the sides of a 9-inch springform pan. Bake for 6 to 8 minutes. Do not allow to brown. Cool on a wire rack for 10 minutes.

Beat cream cheese, 1 cup granulated sugar and brown sugar in a large bowl until fluffy. Beat in eggs, pumpkin and evaporated milk. Add cornstarch, cinnamon and nutmeg; beat well. Pour into crust. Bake for 55 to 60 minutes, until edge is set but center still moves slightly.

For topping, combine sour cream, granulated sugar and vanilla in a small bowl; mix well. Spread over surface of warm cheesecake. Bake for 5 minutes. Cool on a wire rack. Refrigerate for several hours or overnight. Remove side of springform pan to serve.

PUMPKIN TOFFEE CHEESECAKE

Servings: 10-12

This is a delicious change from the traditional pumpkin pie and whipped cream, and is much easier than it sounds to prepare. Shortbread cookies make an excellent crust.

1¾ cups (14–16) crushed
   shortbread cookies
1 tbs. butter or margarine,
   melted
24 oz. cream cheese, softened
1¼ cups brown sugar, packed
1 can (15 oz.) pumpkin
⅔ cup (5 oz. can) evaporated
   milk
2 large eggs

2 tbs. cornstarch
½ tsp. cinnamon
1 cup (about 25–30) crushed
   toffee candies
1 cup sour cream, room
   temperature
2 tbs. granulated sugar
½ tsp. vanilla extract
caramel ice cream topping,
   optional

Heat oven to 350°. Combine cookie crumbs and butter in small bowl. Press onto bottom and 1 inch up around the sides of a 9-inch springform pan. Bake for 6 to 8 minutes. Do not allow to brown. Cool on a wire rack for 10 minutes.

Heat cream cheese and brown sugar in a large bowl until creamy. Add pumpkin, evaporated milk, eggs, cornstarch and cinnamon; beat well. Pour into crust. Bake for 60 to 65 minutes, or until edge is set but center still moves slightly. Remove from oven; top with toffee candy pieces.

Combine sour cream, granulated sugar and vanilla extract in a small bowl; mix well. Spread over warm cheesecake. Bake for 8 minutes. Cool completely in pan on a wire rack. Refrigerate for several hours or overnight. Remove side of springform pan to serve. Drizzle with caramel topping before serving .

PUMPKIN CRÈME BRÛLÉE

Servings: 12

Crème Brûlée is a rich French cream and vanilla-flavored custard. The literal translation is "burnt cream," which refers to the scalded cream or milk in the recipe.

3 cups milk
5 eggs, lightly beaten
1½ cups canned pumpkin or
  Pumpkin Puree, page 3
1 cup light brown sugar, packed

3 tbs. unsalted butter or
  margarine, melted
1½ tsp. pumpkin pie spice
1½ tsp. vanilla extract
½ cup sugar, divided

Heat oven to 350°. In a small saucepan, heat milk to just below boiling. Bubbles will form all over the surface (scalded milk is heated to 180° to 185°).

In a medium bowl, lightly beat eggs with a wire whisk. Add pumpkin, brown sugar, butter, spice and vanilla. Mix until well

blended. Gradually whisk in hot milk. Mix well until all ingredients are combined.

Evenly divide pumpkin mixture among 12 six-ounce custard cups. Place cups in two 9 x 13-inch pans. Place pans on oven rack and add hot tap water to pans until water is halfway up side of cups.

Bake for 35 to 40 minutes. Check after 35 minutes. Custard centers should be slightly wobbly. Remove custard from oven and allow to cool in water bath. Cover with plastic wrap and refrigerate.

Just before serving, Heat oven broiler. Sprinkle 2 tsp. sugar on each custard. Arrange on baking sheet and place under hot broiler. Broil until sugar melts and bubbles. Watch closely to prevent burning. Sugar should be lightly brown and caramelized. Or hold a propane kitchen torch (also called a salamander) about 2 inches from custard tops to caramelize sugar. Serve at once. Refrigerate leftovers for up to 5 days.

PUMPKIN PIE CRUNCH

Here's a classic pie recipe that has been around for over 60 years.

2 cups *Pumpkin Puree,* page 3, or canned pumpkin	3 eggs
1 can (12 oz.) evaporated milk	1 box of yellow cake mix
1½ cups sugar	1 cup chopped pecans
4 tsp. pumpkin pie spice	1 cup melted butter

Mix pumpkin, evaporated milk, sugar, spice, and eggs in a large bowl until well blended.

Pour into a well greased 9 x 13-inch pan. Sprinkle cake mix over top of pumpkin mixture and add pecans on top. Drizzle 1 cup of melted butter over the entire top.

Bake at 350° for 50 to 55 minutes. Cool.

PIES AND DESSERTS

THE GREAT PUMPKIN DESSERT

Servings: 12

Remember pudding cakes? This is something like that—moist, gooey sweet pumpkin pie at the bottom and cake on top. It's the best. And it's so easy! Serve with ice cream or whipped cream.

1 can (15 oz.) pumpkin or 2
  cups *Pumpkin Puree,* page 3
1 can (12 oz.) evaporated milk
3 eggs
1 cup sugar

4 tsp. pumpkin pie spice
1 pkg. (18¼ oz.) yellow cake mix
¾ cup butter or margarine,
  melted
1½ cups chopped walnuts

In a bowl, combine pumpkin, milk, eggs, sugar and spice. Transfer to a greased, 9 x 13-inch baking pan. Sprinkle with dry cake mix and drizzle with butter. Top with walnuts.

Bake at 350° for 1 hour, or until a knife inserted near the center comes out clean.

PUMPKIN GOOEY BUTTER CAKES

Servings: 6–8

Keep it simple: serve these with fresh whipped cream.

1 pkg. (18¼ oz.) yellow cake mix
1 egg
½ cup butter, melted
8 oz. cream cheese, softened
1 can (15 oz.) pumpkin
3 eggs
1 tsp. vanilla
½ cup butter, melted
1 box (16 oz.) powdered sugar
1 tsp. each cinnamon, nutmeg

Heat oven to 350°. Combine cake mix, egg, and butter and mix well with an electric mixer. Pat mixture into the bottom of a lightly greased 9 x 13-inch baking pan.

In a large bowl, beat cream cheese and pumpkin until smooth. Add eggs, vanilla and butter and beat together. Add powdered sugar, cinnamon and nutmeg; mix well. Spread pumpkin mixture over cake batter and bake for 40 to 50 minutes. Do not overbake; center should be a little gooey.

PUMPKIN ICE CREAM SQUARES

Makes nine 3-inch squares

Pumpkin and ice cream all in one: simple—and kids love it!

1½ cups graham cracker
  crumbs
¼ cup sugar
¼ cup butter, melted
1 can (15 oz.) pumpkin or 2
  cups *Pumpkin Puree,* page 3
½ cup brown sugar

½ tsp. salt
1 tsp. cinnamon
¼ tsp. ginger
⅛ tsp. cloves
1 qt. vanilla ice cream, softened
whipped cream and pecans,
  optional

Mix crumbs with sugar and butter. Press into bottom of a 9-inch square pan. In a bowl, combine pumpkin with sugar, salt and spices. Fold in ice cream. Pour over crumbs into your 9-inch pan. Cover with foil and freeze until firm. Cut into squares about 20 minutes before serving. Top with whipped cream and pecans.

PUMPKIN ICE CREAM ROLL

Servings: 10

This wonderful, light dessert is a great standby at Thanksgiving and Christmas. The subtle taste of pumpkin and the sweet taste of ice cream make the most delicious after-dinner treat.

3/4 cup all-purpose flour
2 tsp. pumpkin pie spice
1 tsp. baking powder
1 dash salt
3 eggs
1 cup sugar
2/3 cup pumpkin

confectioners' sugar for dusting
1 qt. butter pecan ice cream, softened
whipped cream, optional
toasted chopped pecans, optional

In a small bowl, combine flour, pumpkin pie spice, baking powder and salt.

In a bowl, beat eggs at high speed for 5 minutes, or until pale yellow. Gradually beat in sugar. Stir in pumpkin.

Fold in dry ingredients. Line a 10 x 15-inch baking pan with greased and flour-waxed paper. Pour batter into pan; bake at 375° for 15 minutes.

Turn cake out onto a linen towel sprinkled with confectioners' sugar. Peel off paper; roll up cake with towel. Cool on a wire rack. Unroll cake onto a baking sheet. Spread softened ice cream to within 1 inch of edges. Roll up cake again, without the towel. Cover and freeze. Let stand for a few minutes at room temperature before slicing. If desired, dust top with confectioners' sugar and add whipped cream and pecans.

PUMPKIN GINGERBREAD

Makes: 2 mini loaves

Pumpkin and ginger are so compatible that to use them in one recipe makes this quick bread doubly delicious. This is my favorite bread during the holiday season.

1 cup all-purpose flour, divided
1/4 cup brown sugar, packed
1 tsp. baking powder
1/4 tsp. baking soda
1/2 tsp. cinnamon
1/2 tsp. ground ginger
1/4 cup canned pumpkin
1/4 cup molasses
1 egg
2 1/2 tbs. butter or margarine
2 tbs. milk
1/3 cup chopped walnuts
1 tbs. sugar

In a bowl, combine ½ cup of the flour, brown sugar, baking powder, baking soda, cinnamon and ginger. Add pumpkin, molasses, egg, butter and milk. Beat on low speed for 30 seconds, then on high for 2 minutes.

Add remaining flour; beat on high for 2 minutes. Pour into 2 greased, 4½ x 2½-inch loaf pans. There will be a small amount of dough in each pan.

Combine walnuts and sugar; sprinkle over batter. Bake at 350° for 35 to 40 minutes, or until a toothpick inserted near the center comes out clean. Cool for 10 minutes in pans before removing to wire racks. Cool completely.

PUMPKIN NUT BARS

Makes: 30 bars

These bars are packed with healthy, energy-giving ingredients.

2 eggs whites, slightly beaten
1 cup *Pumpkin Puree,* page 3,
   or canned pumpkin
½ cup butter or margarine,
   melted
2 cups oats

1 cup brown sugar, packed
½ cup shredded coconut,
   toasted
½ cup wheat germ
1 cup chopped, salted peanuts,
   pecans or almonds

Heat oven to 350°. In a large bowl, beat egg whites slightly; add pumpkin and melted butter. Beat until smooth.

In another bowl, combine oats, brown sugar, coconut, wheat germ and nuts. Fold mixtures together to form a stiff dough. Press into a lightly greased, 15½ x 10½-inch jellyroll pan. Bake for 40 to 45 minutes, or until golden brown. While still warm, cut into 2 x 3-inch bars. Serve warm or cool completely.

CAKES AND COOKIES

RICH CHOCOLATE PUMPKIN TRUFFLES

Makes: 48

Here is a little twist on a candy truffle. You can make these with coffee liqueur, or, for non coffee lovers, apple juice.

2½ cups crushed vanilla wafers
  (about 62 pieces)
1 cup ground, toasted almonds
¾ cup powdered sugar, divided
2 tsp. cinnamon
1 cup semi-sweet chocolate
  morsels, melted

½ cup *Pumpkin Puree,* page 3,
  or canned pumpkin
⅓ cup coffee liqueur or apple
  juice

Combine wafers, almonds, ½ cup of the powdered sugar and cinnamon in a medium bowl. Melt chocolate chips following directions on package. Blend melted chocolate, pumpkin and coffee liqueur with wafer mixture. Shape into 1-inch balls. Refrigerate.

Just before serving, dust with remaining powdered sugar.

PUMPKIN-PEAR CAKE

Servings: 10–12

Here's a good Halloween dessert trick. Turn this cake upside down—and the caramel and pear mixture appears.

1/2 cup brown sugar, packed	1 1/2 tsp. pumpkin pie spice
1/4 cup margarine or butter, melted	1 tsp. baking soda
1 tsp. cornstarch	3/4 tsp. baking powder
1 can (16 oz.) pear halves in light syrup	4 large egg whites
1 1/2 cups all-purpose flour	1 cup sugar
	1 cup canned pumpkin
	1/2 cup cooking oil

Combine brown sugar, margarine and cornstarch in a small bowl. Drain pears, reserving 3 tbs. of the syrup. Stir reserved syrup into brown sugar mixture. Pour mixture into a 10-inch round baking pan or a 9 x 9-inch baking pan.

Cut pear halves into fans by making three or four lengthwise cuts from the bottom of the pear to ½ inch from the top. Arrange pears, small ends in the center and rounded sides down, on syrup in pan.

Combine flour, pumpkin pie spice, baking soda and baking powder in a small bowl; set aside. In another bowl, beat egg whites with an electric mixer on medium speed until soft peaks form. Gradually add sugar, beating until stiff peaks form. Using low speed, beat in pumpkin and oil. Fold flour mixture into pumpkin mixture, just until moistened. Carefully spoon over pears. Spread mixture evenly with back of spoon.

Bake in a 350° oven for 40 to 45 minutes, or until a toothpick inserted near the center comes out clean. Cool for 5 minutes. Loosen from side of pan; invert onto serving plate. Serve warm.

SOFT PUMPKIN COOKIES

Makes: 3 dozen

These soft, chewy cookies smell wonderful when baking.

2¹/₂ cups flour
1 tsp. each baking soda, baking powder, cinnamon
¹/₂ tsp. each nutmeg, salt
1¹/₂ cups sugar

¹/₂ cup butter, softened
1 cup *Pumpkin Puree,* page 3, or canned pumpkin
1 large egg
1 tsp. vanilla extract

Heat oven to 350°. Grease baking sheets. Combine flour, baking soda, baking powder, cinnamon, nutmeg and salt in a medium bowl. Beat sugar and butter in a large bowl until well blended, light and fluffy. Beat in pumpkin, egg and vanilla extract until smooth. Gradually beat in flour mixture. Drop by rounded tbs. onto prepared baking sheets. Bake for 15 to 18 minutes, or until edges are firm. Cool on baking sheet.

PUMPKIN CHOCOLATE CHIP COOKIES

Makes: 4 dozen

Substitute margarine for butter in this recipe, if you prefer.

1 cup butter, softened
1 cup sugar
1 cup brown sugar, packed
1 egg
1 tsp. vanilla extract
2 cups all-purpose flour
1 cup quick-cooking oats

1 tsp. baking soda
1 tsp. cinnamon
½ tsp. salt
1 cup *Pumpkin Puree,* page 3,
    or canned pumpkin
1 cup semisweet chocolate chips

In a bowl, cream butter and sugars. Beat in egg and vanilla. In a medium bowl, combine flour, oats, baking soda, cinnamon and salt; add to creamed mixture alternately with pumpkin. Stir in chocolate chips. Drop by tablespoonfuls, 2 inches apart, onto greased baking sheets. Bake at 350° for 9 to 12 minutes, or until golden brown. Cool on wire racks.

PUMPKIN OATMEAL RAISIN COOKIES

Makes: 4 dozen

This festive treat is a twist on the classic oatmeal-raisin cookie.

2 cups all-purpose flour
1⅓ cups old-fashioned oats
1 tsp. baking soda
1 tsp. cinnamon
½ tsp. salt
1 cup butter, softened
1 cup brown sugar, packed
1 cup granulated sugar
1 cup *Pumpkin Puree,* page 3, or canned pumpkin
1 large egg
1 tsp. vanilla extract
¾ cup chopped walnuts
¾ cup raisins

Heat oven to 350°. Lightly grease 2 baking sheets. Combine flour, oats, baking soda, cinnamon and salt in a medium bowl.

Beat butter and sugars in a large bowl, until light and fluffy. Add pumpkin, egg and vanilla; mix well. Add flour mixture to pumpkin mixture; mix well. Stir in nuts and raisins. Drop by rounded table-spoonfuls onto prepared baking sheets.

Bake for 14 to 16 minutes, or until cookies are lightly browned and set in centers. Cool on baking sheets for 2 minutes; remove to wire racks to cool completely.

PUMPKIN WALNUT COOKIES

This is an absolute must. The cream cheese frosting gives these cookies just the right amount of sweet taste.

1 cup butter, softened
²/₃ cup brown sugar, firmly
    packed
¹/₃ cup granulated sugar
1 cup *Pumpkin Puree,* page 3,
    or canned pumpkin
1 large egg
1 tsp. vanilla extract
2 cups all-purpose flour
1¹/₂ tsp. pumpkin pie spice or
    cinnamon

1 tsp. baking powder
1 tsp. baking soda
¹/₄ tsp. salt
1 cup walnuts, chopped
2 cups powdered sugar
¹/₄ cup butter
1 pkg. (3 oz.) cream cheese
1 tsp. vanilla extract
¹/₄ tsp. pumpkin pie spice or
    cinnamon
walnut pieces, optional

Heat oven to 350°. Combine butter, brown sugar and sugar in a large bowl. Beat at medium speed, scraping bowl often, until creamy. Add pumpkin, egg and vanilla extract. Continue beating for 1 to 2 minutes, until well mixed. Reduce speed to low; beat in flour, 1½ tsp. pumpkin pie spice, baking powder, baking soda and salt. Stir in 1 cup walnuts by hand. Drop by rounded teaspoonfuls, 2 inches apart, onto ungreased cookie sheets.

Bake for 8 to 10 minutes, or until set. Cool on baking sheets for 2 minutes; remove to wire racks to cool completely.

For frosting, combine powdered sugar, butter, cream cheese, vanilla extract and pumpkin pie spice in a medium bowl. Beat at low speed, scraping bowl often, until smooth. Frost cooled cookies. Garnish with walnuts.

INDEX

Apple pumpkin pie 42
Apple butter, pumpkin 27
Applesauce with pumpkin bread 15

Banana pumpkin nut bread 12
Bars, pumpkin nut 66
Beef stew in a pumpkin 28
Berry butter with pumpkin scones 22
Bread
  pumpkin 14
  pumpkin banana nut 12
  pumpkin chocolate chip 16
  pumpkin cranberry 18
  pumpkin nut 20
  pumpkin with

applesauce 15
pumpkin yeast bread-machine 26
whole-wheat pumpkin 24
Bread-machine bread, pumpkin yeast 26
Butter
  berry with pumpkin scones 22
  gooey pumpkin cakes 60
  pumpkin apple 27

Cake, pumpkin-pear 68
Cakes, pumpkin gooey butter 60
Casserole, Italian pumpkin strata 30

Cheese, gorgonzola and pumpkin soup 35
Cheese, ball, pumpkin 9
Cheesecake, pumpkin 52
Cheesecake, pumpkin toffee 54
Chiffon pumpkin pie 44
Chocolate
  chip pumpkin bread 16
  chip pumpkin cookies 71
  pumpkin truffles, rich 67
Cookies
  pumpkin chocolate chip 71
  pumpkin oatmeal raisin 72
  pumpkin walnut 74
  soft pumpkin 70
Cranberry pumpkin bread

18
Creamy quick pumpkin
  pie 41
Creme brûlée, pumpkin
  56
Crunch, pumpkin pie 58
Curried pumpkin soup 36
Custards, individual
  pumpkin 49

Dessert, great pumpkin 59
Dessert, Halloween
  pumpkin pancakes 4
Dip, tomato-pumpkin
  seed 6
Double-layer pumpkin pie
  38
Doughnuts, frosted
  pumpkin 10

Gingerbread, pumpkin 64
Gingerbread pumpkin pie
  46
Gingersnap pumpkin
  mousse torte 50
Gorgonzola and pumpkin
  soup 35
Great pumpkin dessert,
  the 59

Homemade pumpkin pie
  40

Ice cream pumpkin roll 62
Ice cream pumpkin
  squares 61
Individual pumpkin
  custards 49
Italian pumpkin strata 30

Mousse, gingersnap
  pumpkin torte 50

Nut bread, pumpkin
  banana 12
Nut pumpkin bars 66
Nut pumpkin bread 20

Oatmeal raisin pumpkin
  cookies 72

Pancakes, Halloween
  dessert pumpkin 4
Pastry, plain 37
Pear-pumpkin cake 68
Pecan-pumpkin pie 47
Perishable 2

Pie
  double-layer pumpkin 38
  homemade pumpkin 40
  pumpkin apple 42
  pumpkin chiffon 44
  pumpkin crunch 58
  pumpkin gingerbread 46
  pumpkin pudding 48
  pumpkin-pecan 47
  quick creamy pumpkin 41
Pies, storing 2
Plain pastry 37
Pudding pie, pumpkin 48
Pumpkin
  puree 3
  seed-tomato dip 6
  seeds, roasted 8
Puree, pumpkin 3

Quick creamy pumpkin pie 41

Raisin oatmeal pumpkin cookies 72
Roll, pumpkin ice cream 62

Sage and pumpkin with tagliatelle 32
Scones, pumpkin with berry butter 22
Soup
  curried pumpkin 36
  pumpkin 34
  pumpkin and gorgonzola 35
Stew, beef in a pumpkin 28
Storing pumpkin pies 2
Strata, Italian pumpkin 30

Tagliatelle with pumpkin and sage 32
Toffee pumpkin cheesecake 54
Tomato-pumpkin seed dip 6
Torte, gingersnap pumpkin mousse 50
Truffles, rich chocolate pumpkin 67

Walnut pumpkin cookies 74
Whole-wheat pumpkin bread 24
Yeast pumpkin bread-machine bread 26